KT-579-541

Incredible Insects

John Townsend

www.raintreepublishers.co.uk
Visit our website to find out more information about **Raintree** books.

To order:
☎ Phone 44 (0) 1865 888113
🖹 Send a fax to 44 (0) 1865 314091
🖥 Visit the Raintree Bookshop at **www.raintreepublishers.co.uk** to browse our catalogue and order online.

First published in Great Britain by Raintree Publishers,
Halley Court, Jordan Hill, Oxford, OX2 8EJ,
part of Harcourt Education Ltd.
Raintree is a registered trademark of Harcourt Education Ltd.

© Harcourt Education Ltd 2005
The moral right of the proprietor has been asserted.

All rights reserved. No part of this publication may be reproduced, stored in a retrieval system, or transmitted in any form or by any means, electronic, mechanical, photocopying, recording, or otherwise, without either the prior written permission of the publishers or a licence permitting restricted copying in the United Kingdom issued by the Copyright Licensing Agency Ltd, 90 Tottenham Court Road, London W1T 4LP (www.cla.co.uk).

Produced for Raintree Publishers by Discovery Books Ltd
Editorial: Louise Galpine, Sarah Jameson, Charlotte Guillain, and Diyan Leake
Expert Reader: Michael Chinery
Design: Victoria Bevan, Keith Williams (sprout.uk.com Limited), and Michelle Lisseter
Picture Research: Maria Joannou
Production: Duncan Gilbert and Jonathan Smith
Printed and bound in China by South China Printing Company
Originated by Repro Multi Warna

ISBN 1 844 43518 0 (hardback)
09 08 07 06 05
10 9 8 7 6 5 4 3 2 1

ISBN 1 844 43599 7 (paperback)
09 08 07 06 05
10 9 8 7 6 5 4 3 2 1

British Library Cataloguing in Publication Data
Townsend, John
Incredible Insects. – (Freestyle express. Incredible creatures)
595.7
A full catalogue record for this book is available from the British Library.

This levelled text is a version of Freestyle: Incredible creatures: Incredible insects.

Photo acknowledgements
Corbis pp. 6, 19 top, 23 (Galen Rowell), 24 left (Bohemian Nomad Picturemakers), 34–35 (George D. Lepp), 50–51 (B. Borrell Casals/Frank Lane Picture Agency), 51 (Naashon Zalk); FLPA pp. 5 (top, middle, bottom), 7 left, 8, 10, 12 left, 13, 14, 16, 17, 22, 22–23, 24 right, 26–27, 28–29, 32–33, 35, 36, 37, 36–37, 39 left, 39 right, 40–41; Getty Images (Stone) p. 11 left; Natural Visions (Brian Rogers) p. 7 right; Naturepl pp. 4 (Bruce Davidson), 44 (Premaphotos); Nature Picture Library (Andrew Cooper) p. 9; NHPA pp. 8–9, 12 right, 15 left, 15 right, 16–17, 18, 19 bottom, 25, 30, 30–31, 33, 34, 38, 40, 41, 42–43, 43, 45, 46, 47, 46–47, 48, 49; Oxford Scientific Films pp. 11 right, 29, 42, 48–49; Premaphotos Wildlife pp. 26 (Jean Preston-Mafham), 32 (Ken Preston Mafham); RSPCA Photolibrary p. 5 left; Science Photo Library pp. 20 top (Darwin Dale), 20 bottom, 21, 27 (Dr Jeremy Burgess), 28 (Dr Jeremy Burgess), 31, 44–45 (Darwin Dale/Agstock), 50

Cover photograph of a horsefly reproduced with permission of the RSPCA Photolibrary

The Publishers would like to thank Jon Pearce for his assistance in the preparation of this book.

Every effort has been made to contact copyright holders of any material reproduced in this book. Any omissions will be rectified in subsequent printings if notice is given to the Publishers.

Disclaimer
All the Internet addresses (URLs) given in this book were valid at the time of going to press. However, due to the dynamic nature of the Internet, some addresses may have changed, or sites may have changed or ceased to exist since publication. While the author and Publishers regret any inconvenience this may cause readers, no responsibility for any such changes can be accepted by either the author or the Publishers.

MILTON KEYNES LIBRARIES	
PET	J595.7
576100	28-Jul-06
£7.99	

Contents

Incredible insects   4

Meet the family   6

Amazing bodies   14

Feeding   24

Breeding   32

Defence   38

Scary insects   42

Insects in danger   48

Find out more   52

Glossary   54

Index   56

Any words appearing in the text in bold, **like this**, are explained in the Glossary. You can also look out for some of them in the 'Wild words' bank at the bottom of each page.

Incredible insects

Did you know that 90 per cent of all animals on Earth are insects? Insects are everywhere, apart from in the sea.

Insects are **invertebrates**, which means they have no backbone. Each adult insect has three main parts to its body:

- the head carrying the **antennae**, or feelers
- the **thorax** with six legs and often two pairs of wings
- the **abdomen**, with the heart and stomach inside.

Would you believe it?

- Many insects are so small you cannot see them.
- The heaviest insect is the Goliath beetle (below). It comes from Africa. It is as heavy as two hen's eggs.

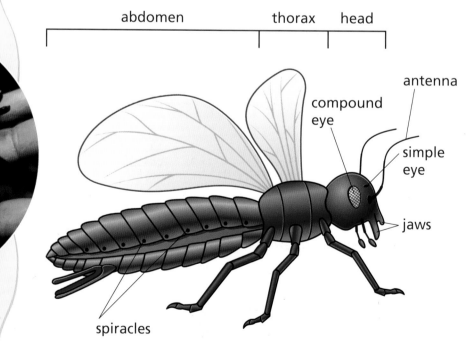

abdomen   thorax   head

antenna

compound eye

simple eye

jaws

spiracles

antenna (more than one are called antennae) feeler on an insect's head

Many types

Some people think that all creepy-crawlies are insects. This is not true.

You may think spiders are insects, for example. But if you count a spider's legs, you will see it has eight of them, not six. So spiders are not insects. Woodlice have fourteen legs. So again, they are not insects.

Animals that are insects include beetles, ladybirds, butterflies and moths, ants, bees, wasps, flies, dragonflies, locusts, and earwigs.

You will find out more about these insects, and many others, in this book.

▼ Grasshoppers are insects. Look at the long antennae on this grasshopper's head.

Find out later...

... how some insects attack others.

... how insects protect themselves.

... which insects are a danger to us.

Meet the family

There are many different groups of insects. They are all different from each other.

Hard wings

25 per cent of all animals on Earth are beetles. For every person there are about 25 million beetles! Some beetles are too small to see, while others are as big as your fist.

Beetles have two pairs of wings. The front wings are hard wing covers that are not used for flying. Ladybirds are a well-known type of beetle.

Colourful insects

People crush up cochineal insects to make a special red **dye**. This dye is used in lipsticks, sweets, and ice cream. Cochineal insects live on cactus plants. They cover themselves with fluffy white wax (see below).

dye substance used to colour something

Scaly wings

Butterflies and moths have large wings that are covered in tiny **scales**.

The best way to tell a moth from a butterfly is to look at the **antennae** on its head. A butterfly's antennae look like thin pencils with little lumps on the end. A moth's antennae often look like tiny hairs or feathers.

Bright butterflies

Many butterflies and moths have brightly-coloured wings. The colour comes from their wing scales.

▼ This is a close-up photograph of a butterfly's wing.

▲ This is a ladybird. It has opened up its spotted wing cases. You can see the flying wings underneath.

scale tiny flake growing from the skin. Scales cover the wings of butterflies and moths like tiles on a roof.

Termites

Termites live in large underground nests in warm countries. Some nests have a tall "chimney" like the one below. The chimneys let out the heat that builds up in the nest.

Ants

Ants are found almost everywhere on Earth. They live in groups called **colonies**. Sometimes there can be millions of ants in one large nest.

Bees and wasps

Most bees and wasps live on their own. But some live in colonies too. Like ants, they work hard to keep their nests clean and look after their young.

colony group of individuals living and working together

Honey-makers

Bees feed their young on **pollen** they collect from flowers. Pollen is the yellow powder you can see inside a flower. Bees also gather a sweet liquid called **nectar** from flowers. They use the nectar to make honey.

Unlike bees, wasps kill and eat other insects. They chew up the insects and feed them to their young. They sting these insects first so they cannot move.

Overcrowded

The largest single colony of ants had over 300 million ants living in it. This "super colony" was made up of 45 joined-up ant nests. It was found in Japan.

► This tree trunk is covered in wood ants. The ants are coming out of their nest in the spring.

▲ These are honeybees in their nest. They are busy storing pollen and honey to eat.

Flies

Flies are all over the world — billions of them. They have only one pair of wings, but are very good at flying!

Flies are useful insects. Many of them eat dead and rotting plants and animals.

These insects can also be pests and spread disease. The bluebottle, or blowfly, buzzes noisily around our kitchens in the summer.

Mosquitoes

Mosquitoes are flies. They are dangerous because they can spread a disease called malaria. The mosquito below is biting through human skin.

Bugs

We often call any creepy-crawly a "bug". But a true bug is an insect with a beak-like mouth. Bugs are found all over the world. They live on land and in rivers and streams.

Bugs vary in length from just 1 millimetre (¹⁄₂₅ inch) to 11 centimetres (4½ inches). The greenfly that attack our garden plants are bugs.

Cockroaches

Cockroaches often live close to humans. They creep behind cupboards and under floorboards.

◄ This is a bluebottle fly. Bluebottles lay eggs on our food and can spread disease.

'Fliers'

Not all insects can fly. Those that do fly come in many shapes and sizes.

One of the largest flying insects is the dragonfly. You often see dragonflies near ponds or streams in the summer time. Dragonflies are excellent fliers.

Damselflies are similar to dragonflies but are usually more slender and they fly more slowly.

Locusts

Sometimes locusts **swarm** in huge numbers (above). Up to 500,000 million insects fly together in a huge, dark cloud. They eat any plants they can find.

▼ Like many dragonflies, this hawker is brightly coloured.

swarm move together in a large group

Springtails

Springtails are tiny insects without wings. Huge numbers of springtails live in the soil. They also live on all kinds of plants. Some do damage to our **crops**.

'Hoppers'

Some insects hop rather than fly. Fleas do not fly, for example, but they are very good at hopping.

Stick insects

Stick insects do not have to move quickly. They spend their lives pretending to be twigs. Praying mantids do the same, but when a tasty insect comes by they can move fast to grab it.

crop plant that humans grow for food, like wheat or potatoes

Amazing bodies

Walking on water

Pond skaters, like the one below, are very light. They have special hairy legs that help them to walk over the surface of the water.

Insects are always in danger. Other animals (including other insects) eat them. Insect legs are useful for escaping danger, but they have other uses too.

Legs and feet

Praying mantids use sharp hooks on their front legs to catch insects to eat. Butterflies use their feet to taste food. They have taste buds in their feet as well as on their tongues!

Hopping and running legs

Fleas can hop 150 times their body length and 80 times their own height! Someone once recorded a flea hopping over 1 metre (3 feet) high. That is like a person hopping over the Empire State Building!

Silverfish are small, silver-coloured insects that live in our houses. They can run extremely fast to hide under the floorboards. Cockroaches run fast too on their long, slender legs.

▶ This is a **time-lapse photograph**. It shows a flea jumping.

Human head lice

Head lice (see below) cling very tightly to human hair using a special claw. Even when you wash or comb your hair, the lice will still cling on. You need a special comb to remove these insects.

time-lapse photograph special photograph that shows the stages of an action that often happens quickly

As light as air

Insects like aphids and thrips (or "thunder flies") are very small and light. They drift about in the air. They can be blown for long distances by the wind.

Strong wings

Insect wings are amazing. They must be light in weight, but very strong. Some insects beat their wings up and down hundreds of times every second!

Fast fliers

Dragonflies, like the one above, are fast, strong fliers. They can fly over 48 kilometres (30 miles) per hour in short bursts.

Hawk moths can reach speeds of nearly 54 kilometres (33 miles) per hour. Now that's moving!

▶ These **time-lapse photographs** show a fly taking off. Can you see how the wings are beating up and down?

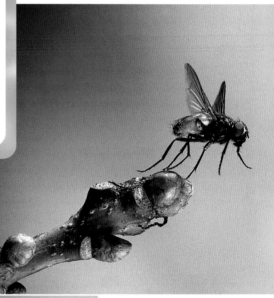

Hover flies

A hover fly is brilliant at flying. It can move its wings up and down incredibly fast. It can hover in mid-air, like the one below. It can even fly backwards!

Flying insects

Many insects are ace pilots. They can perform amazing stunts. Some, like hover flies, can hover in the air. Some can fly sideways or even backwards. Others, like houseflies, can land upside-down on your ceiling.

No wings

Other insects have no wings at all. Lice, fleas, and silverfish are wingless.

Heads and senses

Although insects are small, they often have amazing **sense organs**.

Eyes

Insect eyes are very different from ours. Most insects have two, large **compound eyes**. These eyes are made up of lots and lots of tiny **lenses**. Compound eyes are good at seeing moving objects. Many insects also have simple eyes. These can see only light or dark.

Seeing colours

Flowers provide food for many insects. They often have bright colours or strong smells so insects can find them.

Did you know that plants need insects too? Insects help plants make new seeds.

◄ This bee is feeding from a flower. Its body is covered in powdery flower **pollen**.

sense organ special part of the body that picks up signals, such as scents and sounds

Hearing

Insects use sounds to help them make sense of their surroundings.

Crickets chirp to each other a lot. But did you know that their ears are in their front legs? Grasshoppers and locusts have ears on their **abdomen**.

A cockroach's hairy legs are good at picking up sound **vibrations**. If they feel danger nearby, they escape fast.

Night flight

Have you ever seen moths flapping around lights at night? Experts think that moths depend on the stars and moon to find their way around. The lights in our houses confuse them.

▲ Look at the huge compound eyes of this emperor dragonfly.

vibration quivering movement or fast trembling

This is a male gypsy moth. Its large antennae are good at picking up smells.

Finding the right place

Head lice (see below) use their antennae to find their way around our hair. They prefer clean hair to dirty hair.

Antennae

Insects use their **antennae** to pick up signals from their surroundings. Antennae are often called "feelers' because insects use them to touch and feel.

Insects do not have noses. Instead they use their antennae to smell things. A male gypsy moth has large, feathery antennae. It can smell a female more than 1.6 kilometres (1 mile) away!

colony group of individuals living and working together

Picking up signals

Insect antennae come in a variety of shapes, sizes, and lengths.

Insects that live in **colonies** often stroke and groom each other with their antennae. Honeybees and ants use theirs to give messages to each other.

A cockroach uses its antennae to feel its way in the dark. It can track down crumbs in your kitchen at night.

Heat sensing

Our bodies give off warmth. Mosquitoes use their antennae to sense the warmth of our bodies. Then they fly in for a drink of blood.

▼ This mosquito has feathery antennae. You can also see its large **compound eyes**.

compound eye insect eye, made up of many tiny, single lenses

Breathing

Like us, insects need to take in **oxygen** from the air.

We have lungs to breathe and fish use **gills**. Most adult insects breathe through tiny tubes inside their body. Air enters these tubes through holes in the side of their body. These holes are called **spiracles**.

Under water

Diving beetles, like the one below, live in water. So how do they breathe? They collect bubbles of air at the surface and carry them down under water with them. They have their own private oxygen supply!

oxygen one of the gases in air and water that all living
things need

Insect blood

Insect blood is not red like ours. It is usually a watery, yellow-green colour.

An insect's heart is very different from ours too. It is a tube that runs along the insect's back. The heart beats to swish the blood around the insect's body. Insect blood carries food to where it is needed.

▼ Water boatmen can row themselves through water. They use their hairy legs as oars.

Breathing under water

Lice live on the skin of animals such as elephants, above. Even when the animal takes a bath, the lice do not drown. Tiny air bubbles get trapped in the animal's skin or hair. They are enough to keep the lice alive.

Feeding

Insect mouths vary in shape depending on what sort of food they eat.

Hawk moths have a long tongue. They use it to find **nectar** deep inside flowers.

Houseflies can only suck liquids. They spit juices on to solid food which make it into a kind of soup. Then they slurp it all up through their sponge-like mouth.

Tear moths

A moth from South-east Asia gets a drink in the strangest of ways. It settles under the eyes of cows and drinks their tears!

▶ This is a leaf-cutter ant. Its jaws are like little saws.

nectar sugary fluid produced by flowers

Sharp mouths

Ants have strong, sharp jaws. They can grip and cut up other insects or plants.

Male mosquitoes feed on plant juices, but the females drink blood. They use their needle-like mouth to jab into the skin of animals and humans. Blood is good food for female insects. It helps them make their eggs.

Thirsty beetle

The darkling beetle (below) lives in Africa's dry Namib Desert. When it is misty in the morning, the beetle collects water droplets on its body, so it can have a drink.

Jumping beans

Young moths are wriggly creatures called **caterpillars**. The caterpillars of one Mexican moth hatch inside a bean and eat the seeds inside (see below). When the caterpillar moves inside it makes the beans jump about.

Plant-eaters

Over half of all insects eat plants. They eat leaves, stalks, roots, **pollen**, **nectar**, seeds, fruit, and even the solid wood of tree trunks.

Insects are often a problem in our gardens. They can spoil our flowers and vegetables. They also cause problems for farmers who grow food **crops** such as potatoes or fruit.

compost manure or rotting plants used by gardeners to make the soil richer

Insect gardeners

The leaf-cutter ant does not eat leaves. It cuts them up to make **compost**.

The ants take leaves down into the nest. They lick the leaves clean. The ants then spread out the leaf bits and mix them up with their droppings. A special **fungus** grows on this compost mixture. It is the fungus that the ants feed on.

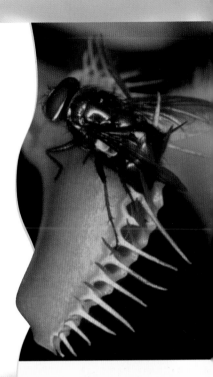

Biting back

Some plants eat insects. The Venus fly trap (above) waits for a fly to land on it. Then it snaps shut leaving the insect trapped inside.

◄ These leaf-cutter ants are carrying leaf pieces they have cut up. They will take them back to their nest.

fungus mould or mushroom. Fungi live on dead or decaying matter.

Predators

Many insects are **predators**. They hunt and kill other animals, called **prey**. Wasps, ants, and tiger beetles are active hunters.

A praying mantid eats beetles, butterflies, spiders, and even small frogs. It stays very still then snatches its prey with its hooked front legs. The mantid starts eating the prey while it is still alive.

Rotting food

Flies such as the bluebottle, below, lay their eggs in rotting flesh. When the eggs hatch, the larvae feed on the dead meat.

▼ A praying mantid waits for its prey to come near.

prey animal that is killed and eaten by other animals

Parasites

Parasites are animals or plants that live in or on another living thing. Many insects are parasites.

Warble flies lay their eggs on the skin of cows. The eggs hatch out into hungry, wriggly **larvae**. They bury themselves under the cow's skin and feed on its flesh. They make painful swellings on the cow's back, called warbles.

Eaten alive!

Some wasps inject their eggs into caterpillars. When the eggs hatch, the wasp larvae eat the caterpillar alive from the inside (see below).

larva (more than one are called larvae) young form of an animal that is very different from the adult

Strange tastes

Some insects eat food that seems revolting to us, such as blood, rotting flesh, and dung.

Lice feed on fresh blood. They can live on us and suck our blood. Lice can even **survive** for up to three days on a dead body. Human body lice can spread disease from person to person.

Blood food

Fleas can live for a few months without food. But they cannot survive or lay eggs without a meal of blood. The flea above is feeding on a mouse.

▶ These dung beetles are rolling a dung-ball back home. They can lift 50 times their own weight.

survive stay alive despite danger and difficulties

Dung-eaters

Dung beetles eat dung. Some gather fresh dung into balls. They roll them into underground nests. The female lays an egg into each dung-ball, then covers the nest with soil. The **larvae** eat the dung when they hatch.

Dung beetles do a very useful job. Without them the world would be piled high with droppings!

Eggs and dung

Flies often lay their eggs in dung. One cowpat can hatch out 2000 flies! In Australia there are about 20 million cows. They each drop around twelve cowpats every day. That means a lot of flies!

◀ These are blowfly larvae, or maggots. They are sometimes used in hospitals. They help to clean wounds by eating damaged flesh.

Breeding

An insect's life is usually short. Finding a partner and making more insects is an important job.

Gift-wrapped

Before they mate (below), male dance flies give the female a dead insect wrapped in silk. While the female is busy unwrapping her present, the male mates with her. This way he can avoid being eaten!

Meeting

Insects have many ways of attracting each other. Male insects often use their **antennae** to sniff out the females.

Fireflies glow in the dark to attract each other. Some flash their lights on and off. Both males and females can glow.

antenna (more than one are called antennae) feeler on an insect's head

Mating

Male insects are often smaller than the females. This can be dangerous for the male during **mating**. He has to be careful the female does not eat him.

After mating, the female insect finds a safe place near food to lay her eggs. This place could be under leaves or in soil, dung, or the dead bodies of animals.

Wood wasps

The **larvae** of wood wasps grow up inside tree trunks and branches. The female wasp (above) injects her eggs through the bark. When the eggs hatch out, the larvae eat the wood.

◄This firefly is glowing to attract a partner.

Cicada nymphs

Insect eggs hatch into either tiny, wriggling grubs called **larvae** or small versions of adults, called **nymphs**. The nymphs of dragonflies, cockroaches, mayflies, and grasshoppers do not have wings.

The mayfly lives under water for up to three years as a nymph. When it becomes an adult it grows wings. The adult may live for just a few hours. Female mayflies have to **mate** and lay their eggs quickly.

Strange timing

Cicadas (see below) are large bugs. Their nymphs live in the soil. In North America, some cicada nymphs take 17 years to become adults.

nymph young insect that looks like an adult in shape, but has no wings

Young mantids

The praying mantid lays up to 400 eggs in a froth of bubbles. This hardens into a shell, which protects the eggs over the winter.

Tiny nymphs come out of the shell in the spring. Their first meal is often one of their brothers or sisters. The nymphs look like ants at first. They grow during the summer before becoming fully-grown adults.

► This is a praying mantid nymph.

"Cuckoo spit"
Froghoppers are small bugs. As nymphs, they wrap themselves in a bubbly froth. This helps protect them from **predators**. The bubbles are often called 'cuckoo spit' (see above).

predator animal that kills and eats other animals

Life cycle

Many insects make a big change from egg to adult. This is called **metamorphosis**.

The female monarch butterfly lays about 400 eggs on milkweed leaves. After two weeks, the eggs hatch into **larvae,** or **caterpillars.**

The new caterpillar is tiny but very hungry.

Do not touch!

The caterpillars of the monarch butterfly (shown below) are brightly coloured. The milkweed leaves they eat make them poisonous. Their bright colours warn other animals not to eat them.

It munches away at the milkweed plant and starts to grow and grow.

metamorphosis change from being a nymph or a larva to being an adult

Changing shape

When it is big enough, the caterpillar changes into a **pupa**, or chrysalis. It forms a hard, outer shell for itself. Inside, the pupa changes shape.

Two weeks later a butterfly crawls out of the shell. At first its wings are droopy and wet, but they soon dry off. Then the new butterfly is ready to fly away.

Amazing journey

Monarch butterflies live in North America. Each autumn, thousands of them gather in southern Canada. Then they all fly south to Mexico for the winter. That's a distance of nearly 2500 kilometres (1500 miles).

◄ This monarch butterfly has just come out of its hard shell. As soon as its wings have dried, it will fly away.

Defence

Prickly customer

Treehopper bugs from Florida, USA, look just like thorns (see below). This amazing camouflage makes them hard for predators to see.

Insects are tasty food for lots of different animals, including other insects. They have various tricks to help them **survive**.

Leaf-eating insects are easy **prey** for **predators** like birds. So, some insects feed only at night when there are fewer birds about. Other insects feed on the underside of leaves, so they are more difficult to spot.

prey animal that is hunted and killed by other animals

Great disguises

Many insects are expert at staying hidden. Some moths have brown wings that exactly match the colour of tree bark. Stick insects and leaf insects look like sticks and leaves rather than insects.

Many insects have just the right colours to make them blend in. This **camouflage** is very useful for avoiding predators.

Keep off!

The swallowtail caterpillar (above) has two large spots on its back. These eye-spots make it look like a poisonous snake. It is a good trick for putting off a predator.

◀ The **pupa** of a swallowtail butterfly actually looks like a bird dropping. But it turns into a beautiful butterfly.

Colours that warn

Some insects have colours that hide them. Others are brightly coloured with spots and stripes. They do not hide at all. Bright colours often mean that an insect is poisonous to eat. The colours say "keep away!"

Sometimes insects that are not poisonous have bright colours too. Although they are good to eat, their colours help protect them.

Colour tricks

The buckeye butterfly (above) is not poisonous, but its bright orange colours might keep a predator away.

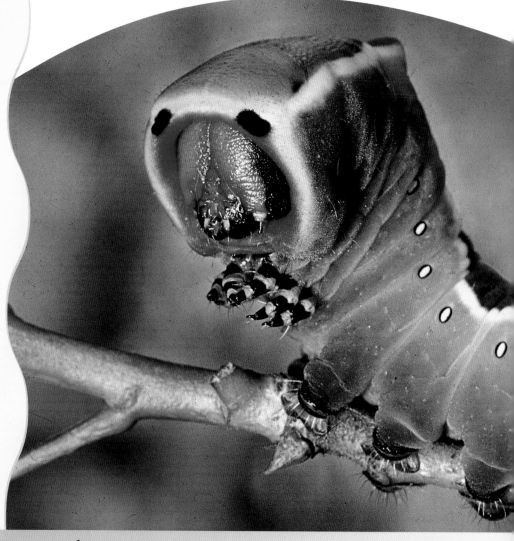

predator animal that kills and eats other animals

Fighting back

One way to scare off a **predator** is to fight back.

Bombardier beetles squirt out a boiling hot spray if attacked. The spray comes from the tip of their **abdomen**. It looks like a tiny puff of smoke. It makes a popping sound as it comes out. The beetle can point the spray in all directions. It is a useful weapon to put off a predator!

Smelly tricks

Another way to avoid being eaten is to smell really bad. The stink bug (shown below) has a useful trick. If threatened, it oozes out a liquid with a disgusting smell.

◀ This is a puss moth caterpillar. If it is in danger, it can squirt out stinging liquid from underneath its head.

abdomen rear part of the body, containing the heart and stomach

Scary insects

We find certain insects quite scary. Some can be dangerous and can harm us.

Tough creatures

Did you know that a cockroach can survive for up to a week without its head? It dies because it cannot drink, and dries out.

Cockroaches

People often think that cockroaches spread disease and live only in dark, dirty places. Actually just a few **species** of cockroach are harmful.

Some cockroaches can spread disease because they go from dirty places, like sewers, into our kitchens.

Cockroaches can live in cracks and crevices in our houses. They come out at night to look for food in our kitchens.

▼ This is a giant burrowing cockroach from Australia.

species type of living animal or plant

Unwelcome visitors

Cockroaches are tough insects. They can be difficult to control when they live in our houses.

They can climb walls easily because they have claws on their feet. Water does not bother them too much. They can **survive** for 40 minutes without air, so they do not often drown.

Ghostly cockroaches

A cockroach that has just **shed** its skin is a ghostly white colour, like the one below. After about eight hours, the cockroach's skin returns to its normal colour.

◄There are more than 3000 species of cockroach. Only about 60 of these are pests, like these American cockroaches.

shed get rid of, or lose

Killer stings

The stings of killer bees are no more poisonous than other kinds of bee sting. The bees have this scary name because they may attack suddenly, and in large numbers.

▲ These killer bees are in Brazil.

Killer bees

Fifty years ago, scientists tried to produce a new bee that would make more honey. But this bee turned nasty.

Some bees escaped and began to spread. They flew north from Brazil and reached the USA in 1990.

The new bees are **aggressive**. Strong smells, bright colours, and loud noises are enough to make them attack.

aggressive angry and likely to attack

Chasing bees

If killer bees decide to chase you, even jumping into water will not keep them away. They just wait for you to come back up for air.

Dangerous stings

Some people have a bee sting **allergy**. This means they can actually die from bee stings. Less than 1 per cent of people have this allergy.

▲ This is the sting and poison sac of a honeybee. They are at the tip of the bee's **abdomen**.

▲ Killer bees have spread up from South America to the USA.

allergy bad reaction to certain substances

On the march

Army ants (shown below) kill and eat most animals that do not get out of their way. Together they can kill lizards, snakes, chickens, pigs, and even scorpions! They can also climb trees and eat birds.

Scary ants

Question: Which animal will eat any other animal in its path and march for miles to find food?
Answer: The army ant.

Army ant **colonies** may contain millions of ants. There is one report from Brazil of a huge **swarm** of marching army ants. The line of ants was 1.6 kilometres (1 mile) long!

▶ Army ants swarm over a forest floor in Trinidad in the Caribbean.

colony group of individuals living and working together

Fiery ants

Red fire ants are also from South America. When they bite, they inject a poison that burns the skin. It can make you feel quite ill.

Red fire ants reached the USA in the 1930s. They travelled there on ships. Colonies began to spread. These ants are now common in parts of the USA.

Deadly ants

The bulldog ant from Australia (shown below) has strong jaws. It bites without letting go. It also injects a poison. As few as 30 bites from an ant like this can kill a human.

Insects in danger

There are over 1 million insect **species** on Earth that we know about. There are many, many more that we have not yet discovered.

For years we have been at war with insects. We kill them with **insecticides**. We destroy the places where they live. We catch them to display in glass cases. Because of this many insect species are in great danger of dying out.

Looks can kill

In parts of Europe, the hornet (shown below) is under threat. People kill them because they look harmful. In fact, they rarely attack humans.

insecticide chemical sprayed to poison insects

Dying out

The coral pink sand dune tiger beetle is a tiny insect with a long name. It lives in Utah, USA. There are only about 1000 left. People take them because they have beautiful, shiny colours.

The burying beetle (shown below) buries small dead animals to feed its **larvae**. If these small animals die out altogether, the beetles themselves are also in danger of dying out.

Disappearing butterfly

The large blue butterfly from Britain died out in 1979. Clearing hillsides for farming left these butterflies without a home. Scientists have now brought them back to Britain, and a small number of these butterflies are living in the wild again.

---

larva (more than one are called larvae) young form of an animal that is very different from the adult

Insect helpers

Insects lay their eggs inside dead human bodies. Insect eggs and **larvae** can help scientists work out when a person died.

Insects and us

Insects can be bad news. In the 1340s, fleas on black rats spread a deadly disease called bubonic plague. The plague killed one third of all Europeans.

Termites eat wood and can cause great damage to houses. Other insects, like locusts, can eat our **crops** and cause **famines** in some parts of the world.

▼ These are Colorado beetles. They are a pest. They can destroy tomato, pepper, and potato crops.

crop plant that humans grow for food, like wheat or potatoes

Useful insects

Insects are small and we do not notice them most of the time. But many insects are very useful to us.

They help keep the Earth clean, they help plants make seeds, and they provide food for millions of other animals.

Without insects, the world would be a very different place.

Deadly curse

Mosquitoes spread malaria, which kills up to 4 million people every year. Bill Gates (shown above) has given a lot of money to help scientists find a cure for malaria.

famine long period of poor crops, no harvest, and no food

Find out more

Websites

Enchanted Learning
Type "insects" into the search box to find links to pictures, activities, and information on insects.
www.enchanted learning.com

Bugbios
The 'Entophiles' pages have fantastic photos of insects.
www.insects.org

BBC Nature
Website with quiz and information on insects.
www.bbc.co.uk/ nature/animals/ wildbritain/ look_around/ insects

Books

Animal Groups: Life in a Colony of Ants, Louise and Richard Spilsbury (Heinemann Library, 2003)
Animals of the Rainforest: Ants, Christy Steele (Raintree, 2003)
Animals of the Rainforest: Butterflies, Eric Braun and Sandra Donovan (Raintree, 2003)
Bugs and Insects Spotters' Guide, A. Wooton (Usborne, 2000)

World wide web

To find out more about insects you can search the Internet. Use keywords like these:

- "dung beetle"
- bee +honey
- "ant colonies"

You can find your own keywords by using words from this book. The search tips on page 53 will help you find useful websites.

Search tips

There are billions of pages on the Internet. It can be difficult to find exactly what you are looking for. These tips will help you find useful websites more quickly:

- Know what you want to find out about
- Use simple keywords
- Use two to six keywords in a search
- Only use names of people, places, or things
- Put double quote marks around words that go together, for example "praying mantid"

Where to search

Search engine

A search engine looks through millions of website pages. It lists all the sites that match the words in the search box. You will find the best matches are at the top of the list, on the first page.

Search directory

A person instead of a computer has sorted a search directory. You can search by keyword or subject and browse through the different sites. It is like looking through books on a library shelf.

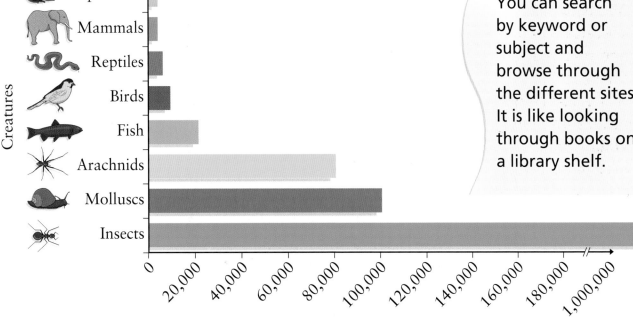

Numbers of incredible creatures

Creatures: Amphibians, Mammals, Reptiles, Birds, Fish, Arachnids, Molluscs, Insects

Number of species (approximate): 0, 20,000, 40,000, 60,000, 80,000, 100,000, 120,000, 140,000, 160,000, 180,000, 1,000,000

Glossary

abdomen rear part of the body, containing the heart and stomach

aggressive angry and likely to attack

allergy bad reaction to certain substances

antenna (more than one are called antennae) feeler on an insect's head

camouflage colours and patterns that match the background

caterpillar larva of a butterfly or moth

colony group of individuals living and working together

compost manure or rotting plants used by gardeners to make the soil richer

compound eye insect eye, made up of many tiny, single lenses

crop plant that humans grow for food, like wheat or potatoes

dye substance used to colour something

famine long period of poor crops, no harvest, and no food

fungus mould or mushroom. Fungi live on dead or decaying matter.

gills delicate, fan-like structures that allow some animals to breathe under water

insecticide chemical sprayed to poison insects

invertebrate animal without a backbone

larva (more than one are called larvae) young form of an animal that is very different from the adult

lens clear part of the eye through which light passes

mate when a male and female animal come together to produce young

metamorphosis change from being a nymph or a larva to being an adult

nectar sugary fluid produced by flowers

nymph young insect that looks like an adult in shape, but has no wings

oxygen one of the gases in air and water that all living things need

parasite animal or plant that lives in or on another living thing

pollen flower's male sex cells, which combine with female cells to make seeds

predator animal that kills and eats other animals

prey animal that is killed and eaten by other animals

pupa stage when a larva is developing into an adult, inside a shell

scale tiny flake growing from the skin. Scales cover the wings of butterflies and moths like tiles on a roof.

sense organ special part of the body that picks up signals, such as scents and sounds

shed get rid of, or lose

species type of living animal or plant

spiracle hole in insect's body through which oxygen passes into the body

survive stay alive despite danger and difficulties

swarm move together in a large group

thorax part of an insect's body between the head and the abdomen

time-lapse photograph special photograph that shows the stages of an action that often happens quickly

vibration quivering movement or fast trembling

Index

abdomen 4, 19, 41, 45
antennae 4, 5, 7,
    20–21, 32
ants 5, 8, 9, 21, 24, 25,
    27, 28, 35, 46–47
aphids 16

bees 5, 8–9, 18, 21,
    44–45
beetles 4, 5, 6, 22, 25,
    28, 30, 31, 41, 49, 50
blood 23
blood-sucking insects
    21, 25, 30
blowflies 10, 31
bluebottles 10, 11, 28
breathing 22, 23
breeding 32–36
bugs 11, 34, 35, 38, 41
butterflies 5, 7, 14, 28,
    36, 37, 39, 40, 49

camouflage 38, 39
caterpillars 26, 29,
    36, 37, 39, 41
chrysalis, see pupa
cockroaches 11, 15,
    19, 21, 34, 42–43
colonies 8, 9, 20, 21,
    46, 47
crickets 19

damselflies 12
defence 38–41
diseases 10, 11, 30,
    42, 50, 51
dragonflies 5, 12, 16,
    19, 34
dung beetles 30, 31

ears 19
earwigs 5
eggs 11, 25, 28, 29, 30,
    31, 33, 34, 35, 36, 50
eyes 4, 18, 19, 21

feeding 9, 10, 12, 13,
    14, 18, 21, 23,
    24–31, 32, 33, 35,
    36, 38, 42, 46, 50
feet 14, 43
fireflies 32, 33
fleas 13, 15, 17, 30, 50
flies 5, 10, 11, 16, 17,
    24, 27, 28, 29, 31,
    32, 34
flying 6, 7, 10, 12, 13,
    16–17, 21, 37

grasshoppers 5, 19, 34

heart 4, 23
hornets 48
houseflies 17, 24
humans and insects 5,
    6, 10, 11, 13, 15, 18,
    19, 20, 21, 23, 25,
    26, 30, 31, 42–43,
    44, 45, 47, 48, 49,
    50–51

insecticides 48

jaws 4, 24, 25, 47
jumping beans 26

ladybirds 5, 6, 7
larvae 28, 29, 31, 33,
    34, 36, 49, 50
legs 4, 5, 14–15, 19,
    23, 28
lice 15, 17, 20, 23, 30
locusts 5, 12, 19, 50

mantids 13, 14, 28, 35
mayflies 34
metamorphosis 36
mosquitoes 10, 21,
    25, 51
moths 5, 7, 16, 19,
    20, 24, 26, 39, 41
mouths 11, 24, 25

nests 8, 9, 27, 31
nymphs 34, 35

parasites 29
poison 36, 39, 40, 44,
    45, 47
predators 28, 35, 38,
    39, 40, 41
prey 28, 38
pupa 37, 39

scales 7
sense organs 18–21
silverfish 15, 17
skin 7, 43
spiders 5, 28
spiracles 4, 22
springtails 13
stick insects 13, 39
stings 9, 44, 45
stomach 4

termites 8, 50
thorax 4
tongues 14, 24

wasps 5, 8, 9, 28, 29,
    33
wings 4, 6, 7, 10, 13,
    16–17, 34, 37, 39
woodlice 5